SECRETS OF THE ANIMAL WORLD

PRIMATES
A Higher Intelligence

by Eulalia García

Illustrated by Gabriel Casadevall and Ali Garousi

Gareth Stevens Publishing
MILWAUKEE

For a free color catalog describing Gareth Stevens' list of high-quality books and multimedia programs, call 1-800-542-2595 (USA) or 1-800-461-9120 (Canada). Gareth Stevens Publishing's Fax: (414) 225-0377. See our catalog, too, on the World Wide Web: http://gsinc.com

The editor would like to extend special thanks to Jan W. Rafert, Curator of Primates and Small Mammals, Milwaukee County Zoo, Milwaukee, Wisconsin, for his kind and professional help with the information in this book.

Library of Congress Cataloging-in-Publication Data

García, Eulalia.
   [Mono. English]
   Primates: a higher intelligence / by Eulalia García ; illustrated by Gabriel Casadevall and Ali Garousi.
     p. cm. – (Secrets of the animal world)
   Includes bibliographical references and index.
   Summary: Examines the different types of primates, their habitats, behavior, family life, and locomotion.
   ISBN 0-8368-1649-8 (lib. bdg.)
   1. Primates–Juvenile literature. [1. Primates.] I. Casadevall, Gabriel, ill. II. Garousi, Ali, ill. III. Title. IV. Series.
QL737.P9G1513 1997
599.8–dc21   97-8489

This North American edition first published in 1997 by
Gareth Stevens Publishing
1555 North RiverCenter Drive, Suite 201
Milwaukee, Wisconsin 53212 USA

This U.S. edition © 1997 by Gareth Stevens, Inc. Created with original © 1993 Ediciones Este, S.A., Barcelona, Spain. Additional end matter © 1997 by Gareth Stevens, Inc.

Series editor: Patricia Lantier-Sampon
Editorial assistants: Diane Laska, Rita Reitci

Printed in the United States of America

1 2 3 4 5 6 7 8 9 01 00 99 98 97

CONTENTS

THE WORLD OF PRIMATES

Where primates live

Monkeys belong to the scientific order Primates, to which humans also belong. Monkeys live in warm, humid regions, such as tropical jungles and rain forests, where insects, fruit, and leaves are abundant all year round, and also because they are adapted to living in trees.

Some primates are not much bigger than a mouse; others, like the male gorilla, can weigh up to 353 pounds (160 kilograms). In the wild, monkeys live in Central and South America, Africa, and southern Asia. Only one species

The gorilla is the largest of all the primates. It is a peaceful animal unless it is threatened.

lives in Europe — the Gibraltar monkey — probably introduced to this region by humans.

This map shows the world distribution of nonhuman primates. They do not live in the wild in North America or Australia.

Common ancestors?

Humans share many physical resemblances with other primates. This is especially true of the great apes — orangutans, gorillas, and chimpanzees.

Many scientists now agree that all primates share a common ancestor. At some point, the human ancestor separated from the ape ancestor and evolved, developing hands to make and use tools and the ability to walk on two feet.

Primates evolved living in trees. Only humans evolved to live solely on the ground.

This monkey seems to be trying to communicate.

Trees are the monkey's favorite place. They are skillful climbers.

Types of primates

There are over two hundred types of primates, which can be grouped into prosimians, monkeys, and apes.

The tarsier is a small insect-eating prosimian that hunts at night. It has long, narrow fingers that end in suckers. Each of its eyes weighs as much as its brain. On the ground, the tarsier leaps like a frog.

The ring-tailed lemur is a prosimian from Madagascar. Its pointed snout, big eyes, and ringed tail make it easy to spot.

Big eyes, small eyes, long tails, no tail, bright color, subdued color — primates come in many shapes and sizes.

RING-TAILED LEMUR

GORILLA

TARSIER

TAMARIN

CHIMPANZEE

ORANGUTAN

Tamarins are colorful monkeys with festive tufts, moustaches, and manes. They are agile climbers, mainly because of their sharp claws.

The orangutan has red hair, long arms, wide cheekbones, and a long beard (in males).

The gorilla is the largest primate. When the male reaches adulthood, its back turns gray. Then it is called a "silverback."

The chimpanzee is the best-known primate. It is intelligent enough to solve problems using tools and objects with handles. It eats mainly fruit and leaves.

IN TREES OR ON LAND

Acrobatics in the treetops

Most primates are adapted for life in trees. Their specially designed hands can grasp branches easily and securely, making them agile climbers and jumpers.

Apes have long arms. Gibbons use their long arms to swing. A human's arms, on the

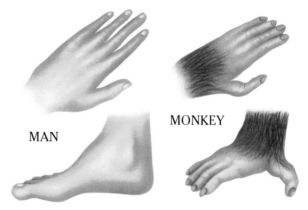

MAN

MONKEY

The thumb and first finger of the monkey's hands and feet are in opposition to each other. In humans, this is true only of the hand.

other hand, serve to handle and hold objects. Humans use their legs to walk on land and support the body. A monkey's big toe is in opposition to, or faces, the rest of its other toes. This explains how monkeys can grip branches with their feet.

Human toes cannot bend to hold objects because humans are adapted to living on land. Instead, the human foot is used for standing, walking, running, and jumping.

The human hand is more agile than the foot. In fact, the human thumb is mobile enough to touch each of the other fingers.

The long tails of some monkeys help them keep their balance. Tails are especially useful if they are prehensile. On the ground, however, the tail only helps keep balance.

The tail is a good safety line for tree-dwellers. Sometimes it is their only grip.

Gibbons are especially gifted at swinging. They grasp one branch after another with their long arms.

Walking on two legs

All monkeys are quadrupeds; they walk on all fours. On the ground, most monkeys use the palms of their hands and the soles of their feet to walk. But some walk on their knuckles, like the chimpanzee and gorilla. Most can stand to keep watch on their surroundings, to intimidate rivals, fight, or reach for food. Young primates, including babies, go through a quadruped stage; they walk on "all fours."

Humans can walk more easily on two feet than other primates. This is because humans have evolved and adapted their bodies to life on land. The human backbone is S-shaped,

The main differences between humans and other primates are the shapes of the backbone and the pelvis, and the size of the brain.

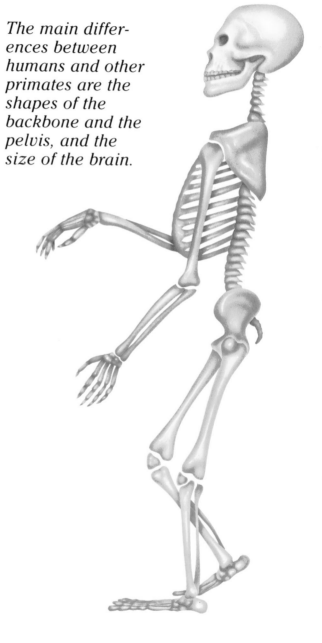

Chimpanzees can use their limbs and even their mouth to collect food and take it to a safe place.

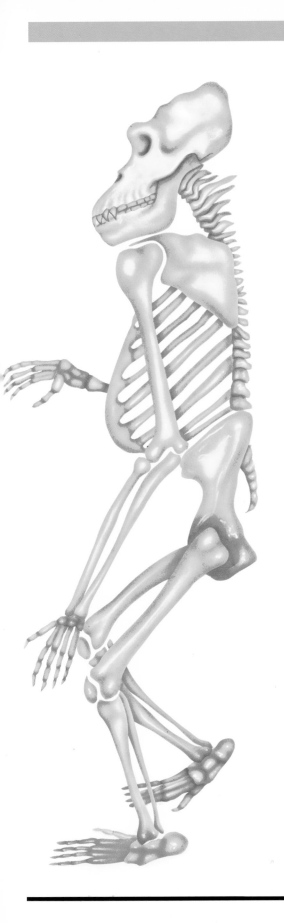

When on the ground, gibbons defend their territory from intruders by standing and waving their long arms for balance.

instead of straight, to make it more flexible. The human pelvis is wider and shorter than in other primates. This makes a firm base to help support the weight of the body.

Of all the primates, humans have the largest brain. Its greater development allows humans to lead a complex way of life, to memorize information, and to be aware of existing.

Humans are quadrupeds at an early stage in their lives. Before walking, babies crawl, or walk "on all fours."

PRIMATE CHARACTERISTICS

Hair and teeth

All monkeys are covered with hair, which is thicker in cold climates. Humans are the only primates whose bodies are not entirely hair-covered. Humans have the same number of hair follicles as other primates, but most human body hair is short, fine, and barely visible.

Apes have the same dental formula as humans. However, human teeth are not as thick, and the canine tooth is not hooked or fang-shaped. Apes have canine teeth that enable them to open fruit, cut bamboo, or to display in self-defense.

Nonhuman primates have few defense weapons, but a good pair of canine teeth can scare off an enemy.

A gorilla's body is covered with hair, except on the face, chest, palms, and soles.

that chimpanzees build nests?

Chimpanzees build nests in treetops, using leaves and broken branches. They make new nests every night. This way, they avoid ants and scorpions and have the smell of fresh leaves.

The chimps are safe from their predators in the trees. Only the huge gorilla sleeps on the ground. However, it, too, prepares a thick bed every day to protect itself from nighttime dampness.

The most intelligent

The brain is the organ that most distinguishes primates from other animals. Outside of humans, the chimpanzee is the most intelligent animal. Chimpanzees can make and use tools. They strip twigs of their leaves and use them to poke into termite and ant hills. In this way, they "fish" for their food. They also know how to chew leaves, which they make into sponges. They soak them in water and suck them when water is scarce.

Although humans can speak, chimpanzees cannot. However,

This is a chimpanzee's friendly facial expression.

they can still communicate with each other by stamping or hitting the ground, clapping, and screaming.

This chimpanzee uses a twig to catch termites and ants.

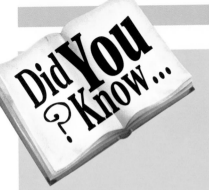

that some primates have a huge nose?

The Borneo tropical rain forest is home to the proboscis monkey, an unusual primate with a long, bulbous nose that can turn bright red. Only adult males have this huge nose. The female nose stops growing before maturity, and the young have snub noses. Male noses grow until they hang over the mouth. Males compete for females, who choose as mates those with the largest noses. Females find big noses irresistible.

PRIMATE ANCESTORS

Seventy million years ago

The first primates appeared seventy million years ago. They evolved from small insectivores. Humans developed because their ancestors found nutritious food sources on the ground. In adapting to new conditions, the human brain became larger with successive generations.

Tupaias are small mammals similar to squirrels and shrews. Until a short time ago, they were classified as primates.

Humans possibly lost body hair as they adapted to life on the savannas, which was much warmer than the forest. Our ancestors were probably long-distance runners, so it was easier to stay cool and eliminate excess heat with less hair.

The first known humanoid was *Australopithecus afarensis*.

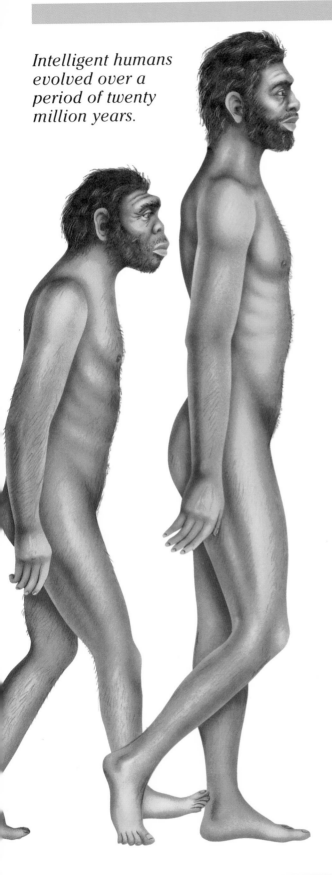

Intelligent humans evolved over a period of twenty million years.

Gigantopithecus, a huge hominid similar to this gorilla, lived over four million years ago. Some say it still exists as the "abominable snowman."

The adult was just over 3 feet (1 meter) tall and walked erect, although slightly bent forward. *Homo erectus* and *Homo sapiens* appeared later. Present-day humans have inhabited Earth for 35,000 years, slowly adapting to the heat, cold, altitude, or sunshine each place offered. This is how the different human races emerged.

that some primates imitate chameleons?

Many prosimians are careful, stealthy climbers. They move slowly along branches, keeping still for a long time, just as a chameleon does. This allows them to hide from predators and prey. Some prosimians are nocturnal. During the day, they cling to branches with their heads between their legs. At night, they hunt for prey, catching them with quick hand movements. They mark territory with urine tracks.

PRIMATE BEHAVIOR

Facing danger

Most primates form groups to defend themselves against big cats, large snakes, and birds of prey. Because of this, it is difficult to surprise them. Some members of a group keep watch from the treetops. When a predator approaches, they warn the others by screeching loudly.

To defend themselves, chimpanzees pick up branches or small tree trunks, which they either pound on the ground or throw at their enemies.

Baboons eat fruit, seeds, and sometimes small mammals.

Adult gorillas beat their chests with the palms of their hands to challenge and frighten their rivals.

Some chimpanzees defend themselves by intimidating the predator. They throw stones or branches, or pound on the ground.

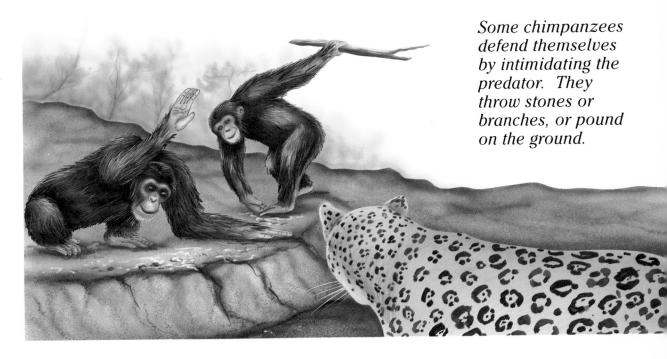

Learning while playing

Young primates spend the day playing. Their games involve chasing and fighting their playmates, doing acrobatics in the trees, swinging, tickling each other, and imitating adults. By playing, the young learn about their world. They learn about their strengths and who their enemies are.

Young primates depend on their mothers for several years. They run to the safety of their mother at any sign of danger.

For this small chimpanzee, playing is fun. It is also a way of learning to prepare for adulthood.

This small baboon clings to its mother's back. It's the best place to see everything and feel safe.

Living as a family

Primates usually form troops, companies that eat, sleep, and travel together. Between meals, the members of a family groom each other. With their hands, they search for thorns, parasites, and seeds in their companions' hair. This grooming keeps them clean and helps maintain family ties and ranking order; the process is hierarchical. Old males, or "grandfathers," receive most of the troop's attention.

Not all primates live in family groups. Male orangutans, for example, live alone in their territory and join females only for mating.

Most primates give birth to one offspring at a time. More would be difficult for the tree-dwelling mother.

These primates are grooming each other after a meal.

APPENDIX TO

SECRETS
OF THE
ANIMAL WORLD

PRIMATES
A Higher Intelligence

PRIMATE SECRETS

▼ **Tiny primate.** The Amazon's pygmy marmoset is 8 inches (20 centimeters) long and weighs 4 ounces (120 grams).

▼ **The siamang.** Both males and females of this gibbon species have an inflatable sac on the neck, which these primates use to produce barking noises.

▼ **The white gorilla.** The only known white gorilla in captivity is Snowflake (Copito de Nieve) in a zoo in Barcelona, Spain.

First steps. Scientists believe small humans walked nearly erect on Earth 3.5 million years ago. Their footprints were preserved in volcanic ash.

Human habits. Some groups of Japanese macaques have recently begun to wash roots before eating them. Members of other groups have begun to bathe in warm waters.

▶ **Bare ears.** The aye-aye is an unusual lemur. It has no hair on its ears, and it finds food — larvae and insects — on others of its own species. They do this by using their long fingers, especially their third finger, which is extra long.

Fat reserve. The mouse lemur and the dwarf lemur store fat in their tails. Dwarf lemurs are the only primates that hibernate.

1. Where do monkeys not live in the wild?
   a) In South America.
   b) In Australia.
   c) In Africa.

2. Why are monkeys good climbers?
   a) Their thumbs are in opposition.
   b) Their big toes are in opposition.
   c) Both their thumbs and their big toes are in opposition.

3. Which primate has an inflatable sac on its neck to make sounds?
   a) The ring-tailed lemur.
   b) The siamang.
   c) The aye-aye.

4. A human's backbone . . .
   a) is straight.
   b) is very rigid.
   c) is S-shaped.

5. Chimpanzees build nests . . .
   a) to sleep in.
   b) to look after their young in.
   c) only once in their lifetime, and they always use the same one.

6. What is the purpose of grooming in a primate family?
   a) To keep each other clean and maintain family ties.
   b) To challenge attackers.
   c) To amuse themselves.

The answers to PRIMATE SECRETS questions are on page 32.

GLOSSARY

adapt: to change behavior or adjust needs in order to survive in changing conditions.

adequate: just enough of anything.

agile: nimble; able to move quickly or easily.

anatomy: the structure of any plant or animal.

ancestors: previous generations of a family or species.

bulbous: resembling a bulb.

canines: sharp, pointed teeth at the front of an animal's mouth, used for tearing off pieces of meat or other tough food.

chameleons: lizards with an unusual ability to change the color of their skin.

characteristics: traits or features separating one from another.

complex: complicated; made up of many parts or active steps.

dental formula: the kind and number of teeth that an animal has. Ape teeth are similar to human teeth.

digits: fingers and toes.

distinguish: to see the differences among members of a group.

eliminate: to get rid of.

emerge: to appear or show up suddenly out of something.

enable: to make possible, practical, or easy.

evolve: to change or develop gradually from one form to another. Over time, all living things change and adapt to survive or they can become extinct.

excess: extra amount of anything.

flank (v): to be at one or both sides of.

hibernate: to enter a state of rest in which most bodily functions, such as heartbeat and breathing, slow down.

hierarchy: the ranking of a group of animals or humans according to power or authority.

humanoid: having some of the characteristics of a human.

humid: damp; moist.

inflatable: able to be filled with air or gas and expand.

influence: to have an effect on the condition or development of someone or something.

insectivores: animals that eat only insects.

intimidate: to frighten, or make timid or fearful.

introduce: to bring in for the first time.

intruder: someone or something that trespasses or enters without invitation or permission.

jungle: tangled, brushy tropical growth.

larva (*pl* larvae): the wingless, wormlike form of a newly-hatched insect; the stage that comes after the egg but before full development.

mate (*v*): to join together (animals) to produce young; to breed a male and a female.

maturity: full development.

mobile: able to move around or be moved freely.

nocturnal: active mostly at night.

nutritious: capable of helping in growth and development.

opposition: against or opposite; a digit in opposition to others can easily touch another to handle or pick up objects.

order: a scientific classification below the class and above the family. The Primate order of mammals includes prosimians, apes, monkeys, and humans.

organ: a plant or animal structure made up of cells and tissues that have a specific purpose, such as the heart, liver, or brain.

parasite: a plant or animal that lives in or on another organism.

predators: animals that kill and eat other animals.

prehensile: adapted for seizing or grasping something.

prey: animals that are hunted and killed for food by other animals.

rivals: two or more individuals that compete with one another for advantages, such as food, territory, or mates.

sac: a part of a plant or animal that is like a bag or pouch.

savanna: a flat landscape or plain, usually covered with coarse grasses and scattered trees.

scorpions: animals related to spiders, which have two large pincers and a long, curved tail with a poisonous stinger.

subdued: lacking in force, intensity, or strength.

territory: an area occupied by one or several of the same kind of animal that is used for foraging and often includes sites for nests or dens.

tropical: belonging to the tropics, or the region centered on the equator and lying between the Tropic of Cancer (23.5 degrees north of the equator) and the Tropic of Capricorn (23.5 degrees south of the equator). This region is typically very hot and humid.

vital: necessary to the maintenance of life.

ACTIVITIES

◆ Mountain gorillas are an endangered species. War in their homeland has increased the threat of their extinction. From library books and the Internet, find out what other dangers these unique animals face. What can people do to help them survive?

◆ Some chimpanzees have learned American Sign Language and are able to interact with their trainers in this way. Do some research on the Internet and at the library on this topic. From your findings, do you think it is possible that primates may someday be able to speak a human-like language?

◆ Visit the zoo and observe the monkeys. Select three or four monkeys and watch each one long enough to get an idea of its activities. Write down your observations. How do monkeys play among themselves? Do you think they have a sense of humor? Do they like to trick one another? In what ways do monkeys show their curiosity?

MORE BOOKS TO READ

Amazing Monkeys. Scott Steedman (Knopf Books for Young Readers)
Apes. Animal Families series. Annemarie Schmidt and Christian R.
    Schmidt (Gareth Stevens)
How to Speak Chimpanzee. Richard Brassey (Crown Books)
The Monkey and the Ape: Close Relatives. Malcolm Penny (Garrett
    Educational Corporation)
Monkeys. Don Rothaus (Childs World)
Monkeys and Apes. Joanne Mattern (Troll Communications)
Old World Monkeys. Wildlife Education, Ltd. Staff (Wildlife Education)
Primates: Apes, Monkeys, Prosimians. Thane Maynard (Franklin Watts)
World of the Mountain Gorillas (3 vols.). Virginia Harrison and Rita
    Ritchie (Gareth Stevens)

VIDEOS

Gorilla. (National Geographic)
The Monkey. (Barr Films)
Monkeys. (Film Ideas)
Monkeys and Apes. (Phoenix/BFA Film and Video)
Orangutans. (Rainbow Educational Media)

PLACES TO VISIT

Cherry Brook Zoo
Rockwood Park
Sandy Point Road
St. John, New Brunswick
E2K 5H9

Royal Melbourne
    Zoological Gardens
Elliot Avenue
Parkville, Victoria
Australia   3052

Fort Worth Zoo
1989 Colonial Parkway
Fort Worth, TX 76110

Milwaukee County Zoo
10001 W. Bluemound Road
Milwaukee, WI   53226

Wellington Zoo
Newtown, New Zealand

Calgary Zoo
1300 Zoo Road
Calgary, Alberta
T2V 7E6

Perth Zoological
    Gardens
South Perth, WA
Australia

INDEX

Answers to PRIMATE SECRETS questions:

1. b
2. c
3. b
4. c
5. a
6. a
